OVER THE MOON

Imtiaz Dharker

OVER THE MOON

*For Jessica
for how we live
Imtiaz Dharker*

BLOODAXE BOOKS

Poems & drawings copyright © Imtiaz Dharker 2014

ISBN: 978 1 78037 120 7

First published 2014 by
Bloodaxe Books Ltd,
Eastburn,
South Park,
Hexham,
Northumberland NE46 1BS.

Reprinted 2016 (twice)

www.bloodaxebooks.com
For further information about Bloodaxe titles
please visit our website or write to
the above address for a catalogue.

Supported using public funding by
**ARTS COUNCIL
ENGLAND**

Cover design: Neil Astley & Pamela Robertson-Pearce.

Printed in Great Britain by Bell & Bain Limited, Glasgow, Scotland, on
acid-free paper sourced from mills with FSC chain of custody certification.

CONTENTS

the telegraM
cAme.
i Read it.
death we expeCt
but all wE get
is Life

JOHN CAGE
for Marcel Duchamp

Like that only

At the sign of the black flip-flop
crossed off in red, by the door
of the Ganesh temple, you are obliged
to take off your shoes, and this you do.

In the face of all the silent watchers
on the steps, you bend, struggle
to undo the laces and come up pink,
not, as a stranger might think,

out of embarrassment. No, you point
at your foot in its black sock,
and there, escaping it,
the pale slug of your naked toe.

You laugh because you know,
as all the watchers do,
that this is the way of things.
A sock inside a shoe is deemed

immaculate. A sock exposed
to public view, especially on its way
to god, will grow a hole.
Even the master of symmetry knew

this to be true. When Gabriel
and the dove fly in, the fabric of the day
wears thin and frays
around the virgin's face.

Light folds itself over a boy's head
and he is shirtless, shivering,
but believes the Baptist will turn
from the main event before too long

to tend to him. You
make a kind of offering
of frailty, an opening for the world
to show its grace

and as you point, the watchers,
children, street-dogs, bottom-scratchers
become your family. You
are a foreigner nowhere.

On imperfect feet, you go in to meet the gods,
the open-armed, the many-eyed,
the asymmetric, belly-shaking gods.

Taal

This music will not sit in straight lines.
The notes refuse to perch on wires

but move in rhythm with the dancer
round the face of the clock,
through the dandelion head of time.

We feel blown free, but circle back
to be in love, to touch and part
and meet again, spun

past the face of the moon, the precise
underpinning of stars. The cycle begins
with one and ends with one,

dha dhin dhin dha. There must be
other feet in step with us, an underbeat,
a voice that keeps count, not yours or mine.

This music is playing us.
We are playing with time.

Bombil, Bumla, Bummalo

At Britannia Café on Ballard Estate
late one afternoon, the poet
was discovered buying Bombay Duck
to take away, waiting to have it wrapped up
in a brown paper bag before he carried it home
fresh-fried and hot. This was where, by chance,
you met.

Simon Rhys Powell and Arun Kolatkar
sat on bentwood chairs and talked
about the art of frying and eating Bombay Duck,
how the bones were soft and melted
down the throat, how it could be swallowed
whole, with *limba-cha-ras*,
just like that.

The poet smacked his lips, you ate his words
as if they were Welsh, both of you savoured
the name itself, the taste on your tongues
of Bombil, Bummalo, Bombay Duck.
Two strange fish swimming in the mirrors of the café
like long-lost friends, bosom-buddies
brought together by a stroke
of luck.

Two lives too big to be packed away
in a brown paper bag like a take away,
you will stay, you will still be there
on Ballard Estate when the boxwallahs
have come and the boxwallahs
have gone.

You will always be there in the mirrors
of Britannia Café, where you swallow life
whole, put your heads back and laugh
at how daft this thing is, not a fowl
but a fish, a dish named for a city,
Bombil, Bumla, Bummalo, Bombay
Duck.

Jurassic

Waking to Jurassic sounds
of crows above the banyan trees,
the distant hawking, spitting, radios
switched on, a hundred stereo TVs,

our bodies afloat in underwater light
and the night a foreign country, this

is how we learn each other, half-asleep,
in a language that invents itself
again at dawn, sometimes remembers itself,
sometimes forgets, and surprises us,
calling out at windows we have left wide open.

Number 106

We are waving to you from up here,
from the fourth floor to say
don't worry about us, we are fine.
We may be strung out, trousers vest blouse
sari skirt on this washing line
but the sun is being kind to us.
Better here than down there
where you are passing
on the Number 106, crammed
into a hot window frame
with your loud loneliness.

We are floating here,
our hearts filled with soft evening air
and the sound of conversations
in the rooms behind us,
in love with the shape
of each other and the dance
we make together,

waving to you, sending a sign
that you would see if
you were looking but

you are not.

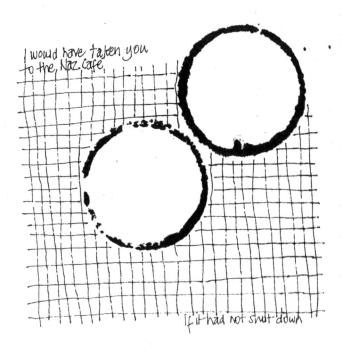

I would have taken you
to the Naz cafe,

if it had not shut down

Hiraeth, Old Bombay

I would have taken you to the Naz Café
if it had not shut down.
I would have taken you to the Naz Café
for the best view and the worst food in town.

We would have drunk flat beer and cream soda
and sweated on plastic chairs at the Naz Café.
We would have looked down over the dusty trees
at cars creeping along Marine Drive, round the bay
to Eros Cinema and the Talk of the Town.

We would have held hands in the Naz Café
over sticky rings on the table-top,
knee locked on knee at the Naz Café,
while we admired the distant Stock Exchange,
Taj Mahal Hotel, Sassoon Dock, Gateway.

We would have nursed a drink at the Naz Café
and you would have stolen a kiss from me.
We would have lingered in the Naz Cafe
till the day slid off the map into the Arabian sea.

I would have taken you to Bombay
if its name had not slid into the sea.
I would have taken you to the place called Bombay
if it were still there and if you were still here,
I would have taken you to the Naz café.

Wild

I go looking for the stories you told me,
the ones I only half-remember because
I was only half-listening at the time.

I leave the city in search of blackberries
to pick off hedges and bake in a pie,
hoping that when it is opened you will begin,
in a blackbird voice, to sing.

Down the lane there is nothing,
but at last in Nannerch, behind the Cherry Pie,
high-heels sinking in the mud and stung
by thorns, I find wild raspberries.
You stretch a frayed sleeve through the hedgerow

into the sun and open your grimy small boy's hand
to let me see the treasure, slightly squashed.
I take the berries from your palm
and eat them one by one. Your days
sing in my mouth, the fruit still warm.

Gobstopper

He rises up off the dump like rising damp,
with a reek that comes at you
out of the swamp of his face, and fixes you
with his glittering eye.

You are only a boy, but a boy
with coins in your pockets, shillings that jingle
up Vale Street and give you away
as a man of means.

He leans into you, cranking his bones down
from a height, his stare so close
you can see the hair in his nose, and catches
your elbow in one skinny hand.

You anticipate the demand he will make
and shake your head, denying the coins
you have saved for a *Beano*, a gobstopper,
aniseed balls, Parma violets and Spangles.

He rears up and hisses. They say
he is a vampire, they say he killed a boy,
he eats rats when he can't find children,
he escaped from the Mental

so you stand very still when he swoops
back to get you. His hair tangles with yours.

If ye caan't help a mate with a pound
when he's down, yer a fuckin' shithead.

He turns away, done with you, thirsty
to drink the blood of something, a rat
or a bat, and you are sprung like a rat
out of a trap, gone like a rat

up a down-spout. When you burst
into the shop the bell jangles
so hard Mrs Williams is warned
that you won't help a mate

with a pound when he's down
but the burden is an albatross
you can live with when you weigh it up
against the liquorice allsorts,
the gobstoppers, the Spangles.

Brookhouse

(for Jean's boys)

The stones are stopped, their grinding done.
The sluice gate is blocked, the big wheel still
and the hoist long gone

but its iron ghost
clanks through the mill, up the stairs
to where it turns and turns the small boys

in their beds cold as stone.
Spun on a spindle, sieved out of sleep,
they turn, scattering water and sunlight

back into dreams of the girls
in the Birkenhead Lido or the ice cream
cone on the pier in Rhyl

or the perfect courtyard on a picture postcard
sent from Urbino. Shaken out, they tumble
away from the millhouse

where the chains are still creaking,
through the tunnel, past the cottages
in the grain-dusted dawn, and leap

into opal water.
Jumping the salmon steps, on a hunt
for the master huntsman, they ride

on the backs of the salmon,
four boys flickering in fresh water,
and before you know it they are gone.

In Wales, wanting to be Italian

Is there a name for that thing
you do when you are young?
There must be a word for it in some language,
probably German, or if not it is just
asking to be made up, something like
Fremdlandischgehörenlust or perhaps
Einzumanderslandgehörenwunsch.

What is it called, living in Glasgow,
dying to be French, dying to shrug and pout
and make yourself understood
without saying a word?

Have you ever felt like that, being
in Bombay, wanting to declare,
like Freddie Mercury, that you are
from somewhere like Zanzibar?

What is that called? Being sixteen
in Wales, longing to be Italian,
to be able to say aloud,
without embarrassment, *Bella! Bella!*
lounge by a Vespa with a cigarette
hanging out of your mouth, and wear
impossibly pointed shoes?

Not for the Vroom Vroom Vroom

Not for the speed or the thrill of overtaking
other riders on the Horseshoe Pass,
not for the shiver of danger in the race
over the Clwydian Hills,

but for this – away past Gwynfryn, Nannerch,
all the names of childhood, sticks and stones,
the breath of school desks and wet gabardine –
escape from bingo-calling Rhyl.

Not for the power, but the nuance of being
delivered through light and shade, light
and shade, to feel the rain fall on green
as if green has just been born.

Not for the Vroom Vroom Vroom
but for the dialect of the machine, well-tuned,
well-meant; the accent of nuts and bolts
from the town where it was made,

not unlike the one you have just left,
inflected to let you live the difference.
Under these wheels, the earth
casts off its weight to be nothing

but the dapple of sunlight and shade.
Your life becomes the road ahead.

Waiting for Crossrail

Victoria and Elizabeth, Ada and Phyllis
swoop in from the ends of the city to marvel
at the newly unearthed find. The tunnel
has seen it all before. It yawns, and at its open mouth

these people have materialised like words
it has just spoken, a speech balloon
that blossoms out of darkness. The tongue
is black and can only stutter, starless,

I lived on your street, this baby fed at my breast.
We had names, we sat where you sit to drink and eat.

Between the City and the pit, the builders
and the diggers are speechless, staring into
no-man's land, its accidental inhabitants
written out in rows. The earth knows

the world is many-layered and must be used
and used again. It throws a blanket over them,

but we are the ones who are shivering.
We remember their passing as if it were our own.

We will always be aware of them
coming and going in our neighbourhood.
They are with us, hurrying
to the market, or standing side by side

on the platform, holding hands,
hoping we will turn and say their names.

They have been here all this time,
waiting for our train.

The first sight of the train

Anyone else would be counting the time, sighing
occasionally, shifting their weight from foot to foot.

You stand dead still, a pharaoh in profile,
frozen on a platform in the luck-down seaside town.

Seagulls swoop around you.
Your eyes do not move to follow them.

Your whole body is intent on watching
for that moment when the train comes

into view around the bend.

You never use the grand vocabulary
of warfare, impatient with the thought of *battling*

the disease. The language you use
is the language of the mechanic, tuning,

tinkering, keeping things running. *I'm just off,*
you say, *for my servicing.*

You will not look away from anything.
This is not a game.

You are good at this,
recognising happiness when it comes

along the track. You acknowledge it,
say it out loud. *There it is.*

Rapt

From the twenty-first floor, peregrine falcon watches
the cranes poised to start the day, the silent slide
of light on glass, the cityrise

at dawn, a blueprint pinned
across grey skies, by noon a work in progress,
nightfall an altered palimpsest.

High up on the concrete cliff, she tends
her scrape, the mottled eggs laid in shell
and feather, searches the cityscape

for the expected guest, then shoots out
soundless on a swoop, a piece of slate-grey
torn off a rooftop, flown back up

to wildness, wilderness.
Past banks of glittering eyes,
she dives and rises with the feathered body

in her beak, its heart still beating.
She blinks, surveys her domain, sees its glaciers.
In her eyes the River Fleet still makes its way

down Farringdon Street to meet the Thames.
She waits in a great silence, greater than
the unstarred sky. She blinks again.

The moon comes up behind the sleeping cranes
and the city is not lost, but rapt,
making space for love to hatch.

The City

Hauls itself out of riversilt and swamp,
trailing marshdamp and the warmth
of creatures it has slept with all these years.

Makes itself up in layers, from clay and chalk,
brick by brick of London stock, standing
not on solid rock, but breathing water.

Rises up at Ludgate Hill to feel
the people flowing through it veins,
and still, the secrets in its underdank,

its lanes, Ropemaker Street, Saddler's Hill,
Goldsmith Street, Ironmonger Lane,
a geography of daily needs.

The City maps its appetites, its hunger,
so that even now a woman lifts her mouth
in Bread Street, Corn Hill, Milk Street,

Honey Lane, to taste the names,
and taste the names again.
On Wood Street, a thrush begins to sing.

Then her eyes remember
The colours flood back in.

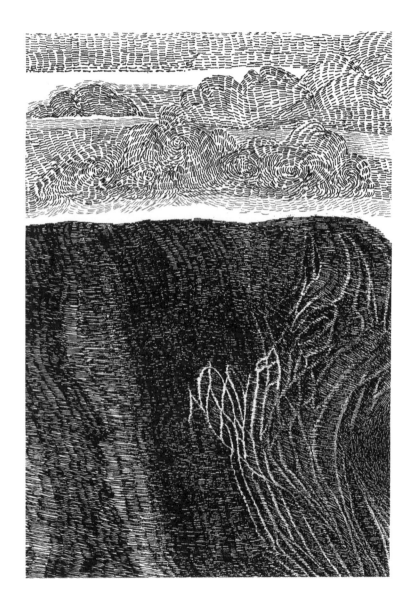

Undone

That tongue of yours is silver when you speak
and silver when the speaking's done.
Those eyes have a look that turns my quick
to silver and proves my body's not my own
but away on loan to your fingers, bold
in their skilful wheeling and their dealing.
Your mouth the alchemist, I am gold,
blown through the eggshell of the ceiling
into a clear Murano sky.
All that goes with me is the scent of you
which could be the scent of me, for there is no I
or you, flung as we are to glassy blue.
    See how well I am undone
      with one touch of your silenced silver tongue

The Appointment

I should have felt the moon
move into the third planetary position
in my chart, and the tides turn.
I should have felt the wave surge,
the deluge on the way, and the boats
behind me burn.
I should have known at that moment
how my luck had changed,
all the lifelines on my palm should have lifted,
spun away and come back rearranged.

I should have known.

But it was Derby on a dull November day
and you were only one more stranger.
You checked your watch and waited
for me, one more stranger,
one door away.

Watching the water

Watch this trick that water does.
It never fails to draw attention
to itself. Every face has turned to look at it

as if it were a work of art.
Each one of these men and women,
though sitting quite apart, is still a part

of the river's audience.
Even the dog has turned to gaze
at the performance

of water-light and the dazzle it creates,
thrown back over the rapt faces,
sprinkled on these lounging bodies,

turning them to legend.
What if behind them, tall towers
are flying flags of smoke

that smudge a perfect sky, what if
behind their backs the sirens cry?
These water-watchers have resolutely turned

away from daily hourly drudgery
to contemplate the dip and swish
of passing riverboats.

Their shoulders and their backs
are washed by light.
They are transfixed,

watching hard but not quite seeing
how blue and orange meet
and take each other by surprise,

how colours can materialise
out of the sky's right ear
and how they can be made

to sparkle
in this trick that water does,
the one the artist knows.

The cranes

The cranes bend their necks
as gracefully as Audrey Hepburn
admiring cut diamonds.

They graze at rooftops,
lift this, place that,
a steel column, a sheet of glass.

Then they stand back
and stop, as if astonished
at what they have made,

a bank of windows,
a counting-house, a doll's-house,
a library, a jewel-box.

Jewel-box

Lean forward at the glass. In focus now,
blurred images align. Windows stacked
on windows, all yours to view
in mirrored symmetry, a choice of lives.

See, there, someone is walking into a room.
Someone in another building altogether
looks round in that direction, seems to speak
right through all the walls and across streets

and streets of separation. These accidents
of movement coincide, the coming in
and turning, speaking, as if it is all
choreographed.

The first one laughs, and the laughter repeats
in frame after frame. Lights switch off and on.
People are sending signals from room

to distant room. They are calling out, answering,
having conversations, passing food,
accepting it, like offerings across divides
they cannot see.

The two moons at your eyes become one.
Windows fill to the brim with light,
the children home, and in the jewel-box,
the pearls still warm.

Alan or David or John

You ask me how it all began. It began
with something unattainable. I fell in love
with an older man. He must have been
fourteen.

His legs were strong. I know this because
he practised cycling every evening, upside down
in the window opposite, and I pined.
Across the street in Pollokshields,
I pined for the boy whose pale legs pumped
and pumped against the dark,
the boy whose name I never knew,
Alan or David or John.

Something about the intimacy of windows, mine
looking into his, his looking into mine:
it never occurred to me when I was nine, but over time
I began to hope for a sighting, watch the black space
until it offered up the gift, the round white face
and then the socks and the legs, the windmill legs
of the boy without a name whom I named
William or Robert or James.

I lay in wait for the sound of his front door,
and before he reached his gate I'd be down the stairs
and out in time to cross his path, red hot under the skin,
but of course he never looked at me and I never looked
at him and I walked past casually, past
Colin or Donald or Sam.

That was when I began to write, hundreds of notes,
a snowstorm of paper, a blizzard of poems
directed to him. He never saw them and never
wrote back, but someone did, eventually.
They sent love-letters to me in books
I brought home from the library,
secret notes for me to come across
in some borrowed golden treasury.

My luve is like a red red rose they said,
Come live with me and be my love, they said,
and they came unruly through the window
of 13 Maxwell Drive to raid my heart
with their silken lines and their silver hooks,
with their sonnets and their couplets
and their wee sleekit words,
Rabbie and Will and John.

It didn't end there. The affair has gone on
for years. Messages still appear for me to find
in books, on screens, in the underground.
I write back. The windmill heart still pumps
and pumps against the dark.

You asked how it began.
It began, like everything, with love.
I wrote and they came, they answered on behalf
of the boy with no name,
Alan or David or John.

The day the marks made sense

When my finger pushed at the marks
jumbled on a page and stumbled
on the word g i r l, when I found
that every scratch had its own sound
g
i
r
l
I said it in Scottish. *girril*
That was just the start. Words
made stories that flew out of books.
Buses had routes and I could
read them. Signs spoke to me
as if they had voices. I sent
messages, word came back.

Then the glass blue days began
and lived in my house as if
they would never crack
or break.

Wean

Wid ye jist look at this!
Jemimah McPherson is minding me
while Ammi is away asking Doctor Gordon
Kerr for a brother for me. She boils a kettle for tea
with extra sugar and milk so we can see who slurps
louder, then she takes a bit of spit to my jammy face,
slams our front door to make a big bang, holds my hand
and runs me fast all the way down Abbotsford Place
to Cavendish Street where her Jimmy lives.

They put me for safety in the kitchen sink
next to the window. The sun is shining so bright
in my face it makes me blink and squint
and squirm around so the light is pouring
over my shoulder instead, right through
Mimah and Jimmy with the confetti of dust
floating around them and the haloes
growing above their heads.

Her pink mouth makes nice shapes and she
looks like an angel to me.
They are laughing and happy. I am too,
because they are looking at me.
Wid ye look at this! Wid ye jist look at this!
Look at the wean wi' a fag in her gob!

My cheeks awobble, spluttering,
Mimah holding me so I don't bang ma heid
on the tap. Smoke in the sunlight, smoke in my eyes,
all of us laughing till we are greetin',
and I am squealing, *Mimah, Mimah! More!*

Ghazals on the Grundig, Pingling in Pollokshields

The moon of the fourteenth day
or the first light of the sun, I swear
to God, you are beyond compare.
The moon...

Out of its massive grey body,
Grundig TK20 is singing reel to reel,
unspooling love songs in Hindustani,
a voice that is sometimes female,
sometimes male. Lahore arrives via Germany
on Sunday mornings in Pollokshields.

What does it mean?
Time, Ammi translates, and sighs,
Time has played such a joke on us
You are no longer you. I am no longer I.

We learn Hindustani from Grundig,
singing along with the tragic song.
Ammi says we must speak English,
Say it like this, excuse me, thank you,

but when I say the words they come out
Glaswegian. To her it all sounds the same.
She finds new ways to speak the new tongue,
delighted by the birds on television,
waddling to the sea, *Pingling! Pingling!*
and the chorus girls who come out highkicking
when the sequined curtain goes up,
Nappy! Nappywali!

Sometimes she lapses, negotiates meals
in Urdu, swears by accident in Punjabi,
Ullu di patthi! But if I am the daughter
of an owl who is the owl?
Grundig's barrel body is rumbling
to release the voice, pitched impossibly high,
juggling the world from spool to spool.
Time has played this joke on us,
says Grundig,
You are no longer you,
I am no longer I.

Nicked

Someone came by moonlight and lifted it
from under our noses. We never heard a thing.
It was smuggled on a ship to Boston, entered
Cawnpore through improper channels. This
pilfering has been going on for years. Creole,
Yankee, Hinglish, Pinglish, Singlish,
some cat has got our tongue.

You can't keep counting the silver
after the guests and hired help have gone.
One by one, bits disappeared, a fork, a phrase, a spoon.
They found pieces of it, years later, in Madras,
Holetown, Kingston, Cameroon.
Then it was melted down and came out
different.

Some cat opened its mouth
and used our silver tongue to sing.
It could have been the Welsh, it could have been
the Scots, but we were the ones they put in the dock
in front of a judge and jury, for questioning.
Did you never suspect it was happening?
Did you look the other way?
Why did you not report it missing?
This looks to us like an inside job.

What have you got to say for yourself
eh? Cat got your tongue?

Speech balloon

The Liverpool boss was pretty chuffed with himself,
said the news report, for being so tough
when he decided to snub the obvious choice
and go instead for the goal machine.
I'm over the moon, they said he said.
I'm over the moon, he said.

The Barnsley manager was lost for words
to describe his feelings when Chelsea fell
to the Tykes. *We played fantastic.*
I never thought we'd do it again
but we did, we did, and all I can say is
I'm over the moon, they said he said.
I'm over the moon, he said.

The Hollywood mum was way beyond thrilled
according to friends, when she delivered
into the world, not one bouncing baby
but twins instead to the astonished dad.
I'm over the moon, they said she said.
I'm over the moon, she said.

Bollywood's hottest couple was proud to be blessed
by the jubilant father, the superstar.
It's a match made in heaven, he said to the press,
Between two shooting stars with shining careers
and I'm over the moon, of course, he said.
I'm over the moon, he said.

The Malaysian nation went mad with joy
on independence day in its fiftieth year
when a doctor-cum-part-time-model,

a local boy, went up into space in a Russian Soyuz
and in zero gravity, performed his *namaaz*.
All of Malaysia over the moon, they said on the news,
twenty-seven million people over the moon.

You must have noticed, it's really quite clear,
this condition has spread, it's happening there,
it's happening here. It's full-blown, grown
beyond every border, to the furthest corner
of every country where English is spoken
or English is known.

There's no one just satisfied or mildly pleased
or chipper or chirpy, contented or cheerful,
no one glad or gratified, delighted or jubilant,
elated, ecstatic, joyful or gleeful.
All the happy people have left this world.
You won't come across them any time soon

and if it's happy sound-bites you're looking for
you need to look way over your head
for the words in balloons

to the place where the cow keeps jumping
over and over
with all the footballers, team managers
and lottery winners, world superstars,
heroes and champions and legends and lovers
and proud mums and dads

and the whole of Malaysia

over the moon
over the moon
over the over the over the moon.

Meanwhile at the Irani Bakery

The lawyers come flapping in like crows
to squabble over neon cake.

From their stake on the pavement, rows
of court typists take a break

for nankhatai and a cup of chai.
Blind from the sun, they hardly speak,

just wipe their damp necks and lift
up their faces, their mouths open beaks

to feed on the air from the ceiling fan.
Under the sign that says,

'Ginger Biscuit Removes Cough',
you cough. The lawyers rake up

small change with their claws
and make off in a flock of shadows.

At the table furthest from the door,
a man whose shirt has been washed

too many times orders more
bun maska. The butter has slid off

the soft white bread to kiss his cheek.
Across the room from him the watching clock

keeps wiping its face
and wiping its face again.

Mumbai? Kissmiss?

Of course! Who is not knowing this,
that after Happy Diwali comes Merry Kissmiss!
Impossible to miss, when allovermumbai,
Matharpacady to A to Z Market, rooftops
are dancing in chorus

and alloversky
is fully full with paper stars.

Hear! Horns are telling at midnight on every street,
Happy Happy Happy! We know very well
to make good festival, and Saint Santa is
our honoured guest in Taj Hotel.
We are not forgetting.

And allovermumbai alloversky
is fully full with paper stars.

See! Tree is shining and snow (cotton-
wool but looks good, no?). Small child also
face is shining, licking icing, this
must be what snow tastes like
under the paper stars.

And allovermumbai alloversky
is fully full with paper stars.

Signs of life

If I were to write a pineapple like a poem
I would look at its eyes to see
what it wanted to be, and then I would make it
what it did not expect to be.
I would slice off its crown
and its thorny skin, slash it and cut it down,
turn it inside out and around.
I would examine it for signs of life,
hold up a mirror to see if it breathed, check
for pulse or rhythm.

If its heart was still beating
I would eat it alive.

If I were to dig up a poem
like a potato
I would root it out of cold soil,
bang it hard on a rock
to shake off the dirt and look at its face
for signs of fight. I would wash it, scrape it,
gouge out its eyes, to make up my mind
if this poem was worth boiling or mashing
or roasting or baking
or cutting in cubes and frying
with cumin.

If I was satisfied
I would give it to you to read
and you might say, *That
was a fine potato.*

Don't Miss Out! Book Right Now for the Journey of a Lifetime!

We plan a holiday, a mini-break, a long weekend, a stolen week.
We trawl the options, seek out the perfect combination of hotel
and flight, the distant beach, the extra night, consider packing
suitcases, examine the travel clothes and lotions, get as far as
tying on our baggage tags. Then I look at you standing here
in this pale grey light and think that I have miles and miles
to go before I know you, and as in any unknown country
I may wish to travel to your sites, and make repeated
visits to become familiar with you. We look out of
the bedroom window at the usual view and think
we may prefer to linger on here, where we have
each other's endless landscapes to explore,
where I seek out your shore, you stalk my
tigers and the world will say it lost us.
This will be our stolen week, your
kiss my break, my eyes your lake
your mouth will be my Paris.
And as for Machu Picchu,
there are other routes
than dizzy altitude
to render us light-
headed, other
ways than
thin blue
air to
leave
us

breathless, and we are here,
not away not far but where
we want to be, still where
we were, this red arrow
pointing straight at
who we are, and

You Are
Here

It doesn't matter

It doesn't matter if the train is late, held up
for an hour or more on the aimless edge of town.
Signals have failed and explanations
are being offered, but we are sitting in Coach B,
Seats 22 and 23, drinking tepid coffee
from the trolley and it doesn't matter, we agree,
it's not as if I am waiting for you or you
are waiting for me at the wrong end of the long journey.

It's not as if you are on a rainy platform
or I am home alone, wondering
if I should call your mobile phone. It's not as if,
thinking of me waiting, you are trying
to get through to let me know.

It is not like that.
Our time is stopped.

Your arm warms mine. We are sharing
a slice of time, time held up
for us. We look at it this way and that,
at its finesse, its endlessness.
We admire this time we have
as if it were a work of art.

Just look at this, time on our hands,
your hand in mine. It doesn't matter,
you say to me, it doesn't matter
if the train is late.

At Smithfield, waiting to get in

All these girls are waiting
in this city and every city
for something to begin,

holding their thin bodies in their arms,
hissed at by cars that pass
in the rain. They are contained

behind the barricade that draws
a metal line between them
and the freezing vans.

At the meat market across the road,
busy men in white coats are dancing
their daily load of carcasses

into patient rows.
Later in the night their coats
will be smeared with blood.

Later in the night
when *Sailing By* is done
and the shipping forecast has begun

thinking of all those souls
out in the dark and cold, thinking
of the ones alone, the others

lying side by side, holding hands,
I remember the young girls
who are younger every day

the ragged line they make,
how their legs are blue
and their faces

lit up before they reach
the light inside,
in anticipation of the dance.

True

(The Bathers, Paul Cézanne)

The women are unfinished. They have
unlikely legs, not quite buttocks, undecided
hips. If it is true that they have bathed, if we wish
to believe that there was water, a pool,
they have emerged as fish,

a shoal dragged on to dry light,
left to sprawl on grass. They do not smell
of water or the underwater. They smell of blue.
Reeking of cobalt, cerulean, azure, ultramarine,
their bodies are approximate.

When they have had enough of being
almost made, made up in this imagined bliss,
they will get up, yawning, strip off their fame,
step away from canvas, leaving
on the floor beneath the frame

no water-drops but footprints, glass.
They will look kindly on their own
improbable bodies, dress themselves
in ordinary, put on shoes and socks,
corsets, coats and hats and plastic

macs. I see them waiting at bus stops
and at railway stations. On the trains
that run almost on time, on tracks
of everyday, they make their way
home through unexpected rain

to where the light comes true,
where free comes true, where blue
comes almost true.

Chiller

It starts with trucks that roar in
out of the night at 2 a.m.,
like giant barns on wheels

and inside, the carcasses on hooks.
You can just see them swaying
and probably singing all the way

from Wales,
or Denmark or Scotland,
a fleshy chorus line

ready to be pushed along
the moving rails to the chiller
where they wait

for their day. Their day will come.

All-night café

The sky has been glassed. There
is a red gash across its cheek

and the heavies have thrown
it, wasted, out into the street.

Still, the city is not lost, even if
it has come out trashed, unsteady

on its feet,
calling for minicabs that never come.

The only home it needs
is the all-night café

where the workers stop
at dawn to eat

when the delivery trucks
have come and gone

and the morning arrives
with a pencil behind its ear

ready to serve up
a fried sun and bacon.

Night shift

She looks like any girl,
but her smile lights up the night shift
in the twenty-four hour café, and this girl,
when I ask her name, says,
My name is Marvellous.

Marvellous. Marvellous.
In my eyes you become Marvellous.

Then I ask, *Marvellous,*
what is your second name?
and she says, *It is difficult.*
I say, *After Marvellous, what can be*
difficult? So she says, carefully,
Makanaka.

Oh Marvellous Marvellous Marvellous Makanaka,
your name is a song, your name should be up
in lights with the great names of the world
where it belongs, Marvellous Marvellous Makanaka

I can see from your name that your mother and father
danced in the streets when you were born
and sent out sugar-sweets to tell the world a gift had come
to them, and they called you Marvellous,
they called you Marvellous, they called you
Marvellous Makanaka.

I wish every father in every country
would look at his girl when she was born
and say, *This one is definitely Marvellous,*
this one can only be Marvellous. Then
they would all be different girls,

they would all have your smile,
that blinding smile,
MarvellousMarvellousMarvellousMakanaka.

Christmas Eve on the Number 4

An unlikely collection this, shuffling
on to the bus at Waterloo, two
with overloaded rucksacks, dangerous
only because they are clumsy and unaware
of old ladies toppling behind their backs,
one with a suitcase of tumbled clothes,
all black. No chance that anyone has packed
the frankincense, no myrrh here.

On the bridge a flock of skateboarders
comes on board with talk of Max and Weasel,
their butterflip or boardslide and the hope
of a calfwrap. At the next stop,
shoppers arrive bearing gifts
in plastic bags with famous names in varied
fonts but no spice or gold for a king,
more likely bedroom slippers

for a wife, or scented candles for the bath.
On a mobile phone, someone is asking
about a child. This bus has no ambition,
it is not following any star, only
the route laid down from A to B,
this far, no further. So passing St Paul's
no one expects a choir of angels
and the bells are silent, saving themselves

for midnight. If there is a virgin
among us, it is hard to tell. But delivered
home, worrying perhaps at how we spent

our money or our time, we take off our shoes
to free our pulpy feet and kiss the one we love.
We were not wise. We did not fall down
and kneel in adoration and yet
we have been saved for this, we have been saved.

I take

I take
>   your body where love takes place
I take
>   your mouth where my life takes shape
I take
>   your breath which makes my space
I take
>   you as you are, for good
I take
>   you with open arms, to have
I take
>   you to have
>   and to hold but not to hold
>   too hard
I take
>   you for farther for closer
>   for sooner for later
till
till
>   death us do
>   death us do death us
>   death tries to get us

>   and we laugh and we stall
>   and we tell it to call us some other
>   fine day because we are busy today
>   taking our tea with buttered
>   hope and
I take
>   thee
I take
>   thee

Gift

In a night made small
by coming too close to daylight,
in a room becalmed
by knowing the calm will break,
I wake. In search of water,
I find you sleeping on a sofa
when I imagined you safe
in the warm bed I have just left.

Shocking, this displacement, as if
in a second, the bed has emptied,
the sofa just been filled
by your immediate body, fallen too white
into a spotlight angled to receive you,
eyes hollowed under eyebrows,
forehead and cheekbones burning bright.

You open your eyes and look at me,
not smiling.
Both of us there, not there, surprised
to find each other superimposed
on empty space.

You, fallen out of sleep.
I, expecting no one. It is as if
from a dark window a curtain lifts
for just one moment
and where there should be only black
outside, a face appears
still and calm,
perhaps a gift.

Ace Café

You head out the usual way
along the North Circular to the Ace Café

to hang out with all the other sad old gits,
you say. You give each other the time of day

over one-pound mugs of tea, exchanging tips
about silencers, chrome or black or chrome.

The conversation you really have
is made of things you do not say

before dusk settles down and you head home,
pale rider displaced in time.

In your pocket the pound coins chime
as you pull away,

your own shadow riding ahead of you,
away from the Ace Café.

A hundred and one

Be old. Be very old.
Wear bedroom slippers and cardigans,
smoke a pipe, grow bald.
Buy a loaf of bread and count
your pennies very slowly at the till.
Eat boiled egg and burnt
toast and jam for every meal.
Complain bitterly about the young.
Sit on the sofa watching telly
till you are at least a hundred and one

or two or three. Be old.
Be very old with me.

Un salon con mil ventanas

Outside with the girls I am waiting
for the queue to shuffle me in
where the spotlight can strip a face naked
for one second before it moves on
       it moves on it moves on it moves on

in the place where our music is playing,
where the heaving walls take us in
and their eyes are the thousand windows
that close and open in turn
       as we turn as we turn as we turn

we are not walking but waltzing
through pauses that lift us like wings,
our feet one two three on the ceiling
and the mirrors watching us spin
       as we spin as we spin as we spin

and there's your head on my shoulder,
at my cheek your quickening breath,
if I don't look back I can keep you forever,
that's how we will cheat
       don't say it don't speak it don't write it,
       don't turn, my love, don't turn.

If I watch my step if I don't look back
if I hold the red rope if I swallow the hope

       if I spin if I spin if I spin

Talker

When there is no one else close by
to talk to, you have this habit
of speaking to yourself.
I can hear you out in the workshop,
talking to a motorbike or to its wheels,
scolding a stubborn saw or drill.

When you sit up in the study
poring over papers in the night
I sometimes hear you discussing
(I think with your first, dead wife)
the question of insurance and electric bills.

Once or twice I have caught sight of you
walking down the street alone,
your mouth moving and your hand replying,
because the conversation once begun
must take its course till it is done,

and every night before the clock strikes one,
over the radio's monotone, you tell me
our whole day from start to end, how we woke
and where we walked, how the time unfolded
like an origami bird

till we came home to bed, hand in hand,
past the shivering queue of Saturday girls
with pale legs and brave faces, their teeth
chattering, their words hung in front of their mouths
as if they were only talking to themselves.

Wiped

All that talk wiped out.
All the words left looking at each other
as if they have no memory of where they came from
or what they are doing here, before
they shuffle away, backwards.
The sound track of a life switched off, leaving
only this,

the low hiss of rain on windows,
electric things on standby, humming slightly,
the no noise that is deafening,
the absence on a page that reads
like ice.

Through the frozen sheets
the mouth opens to speak.

The face breaks.

Listener

It was the time before time
hung, like a hanged man,
when the second hand of a clock
said familiar endearments
in your exact voice, in the exact rhythm
of your start and stop. Time
to be summoned out of a blacked-out room
to listen for you
breathing

at the centre of the house.
The centre of the house

not breathing
but listening, holding its breath
as if black water had closed over its head
and its heart were about to stop
its burdened beating, swung
between the pendulum and your voice
in the clock, heavy as a drowned woman
it was the time before time,
it was time.

Stab

Stab the page. Stab it in the heart.
Find the word that is not a word.
Find the word that is a blade.
Slash the empty space
to fall into the teeming dark,
find the face.

Make one mark.

You said something I did not understand

Get me out, you said. *Now.*
Get me out. The unfamiliar bed
a prison, your body behind bars,
your bright spirit locked away.

I once knew what you meant to say before you said it,
I understood every lift of your eyebrow, every look.
I could read you like a book.

The words play
and play again. As I pay
at a till for milk or bread,
board a train, turn and turn on the pillow
where your head should be
Now, you say

and it slams shut around me, that last day
when I chose not to understand you,
when I tried to keep you, keep you
in my custody, walled in by my will,

when I tried to make you stay.

Vigil

Your eyes open, silver
for one second, close.
Your hand stops, falls still.
You send me no more messages.

The machine by your bed
is saying prayers for you.
It keeps watch, tenderly interpreting
your body's needs.
It listens and records your every breath,
the turning of your blood, your heartbeat.

All night, all night, it pays close attention
to you. At dawn it stops.

I try to read its face.
The machine is blinking back
its tears.

Vroom

This month is the arsonist. It strikes
its match and trees catch fire down every street,
out across the country lanes, all the way to Wales.

No mists here, but leaves cut out of glass
stained crimson, carmine, orange, gold.
Your colours fly from every mast.

You never belonged down in the tube-lit room,
trapped in a web of wires and tubes, and will not stay
a minute longer than you must.

The machines open their hands, lose
their grip on you, and you are gone, flown
ahead of us, along the clanging corridor

up the stairs and out. Out at last
to where the day fires up and speaks to you
in tongues of blackbirds, London buses, cars,

taxis, human voices, trumpets, cymbals,
joyful brass. You head off on Brompton Road
and the leaves are flames

that light you up, your face aglow,
not looking back, knowing this is the way
to go.

After

We have done all the things you
would have liked us to do.

Your brother has been across the country and back
to fetch your comfortable shoes.

We have dressed you in your good wedding suit
and the ironed shirt. Someone has combed your hair.

This is exactly as I wanted it, you will say,
after the tributes have been paid,

when the organ has been played
and the hymns have been sung,

when we have told all your jokes
and the well-wishers have gone,

Exactly, you will say
when you are done with dying,

when you come back home.

The other side of silence

The roar of your leaving dies away
and this is when I hear

the sound a blue eggshell makes
when it falls on grass

or the small splutter
of rain shaken off an umbrella

or the sigh that escapes
the shirt thrown on the floor,

the surprised breath
of all things left behind,

not a protest,
just that sense of being

unclasped.

The closed door

Your shirts are all washed and pressed
waiting for you
waiting for me
to open the wardrobe door.

Rinse cycle

The signs and signals
              make no sense.
Two people across the way
                    are talking but
their hands
          and mouths are saying
                              opposite things,
and both are disconnected
                    from their eyes.
They may as well be
              fish, blowing empty
speech bubbles
            into uncomprehending air.
I say something
            no one seems to understand.
Buses arrive and pause
                  grunt and pass
but no one gets on because
                        their destination boards
are talking gibberish.
                  Since yesterday
even the dishwasher
                is refusing to end its cycle,
but is sending the water in
                  water out,
pushing the rinse round
                  and round,
and is suddenly speaking
                  Swedish.

Medium

All life is out there, spending, spending,
spendthrift with its silver
like a drunk on moonshine.

Across the coffee-shop, baristas
are calling out to one another in Malayalam,
coffee burbles in Spanish,
the streets are a torrent of passing Italian,
windows fly open on Punjabi, doors
bang in Swahili, cars go by in a rush
of German, screens flash off and on
in Russian, mobile phones shout Mandarin,
the school playground is screaming Sylheti.
Even songbirds are chirping in accents,
Valleys, Geordie, Bhojpuri.

This upturned glass is mute, but wants to go
screeching across the table,
its mouth ravenous for word of you.

The world is squandering its currency
of languages.

Save one.
Speak to me.

Presence

Throw out the sad ouija board,
take the moving glass and break
its wailing. Scatter the tarot cards
off the high tower, watch them sailing
down the river. With her flower-
printed bags, send the medium packing
back to Brighton or Frinton or wherever
it was she came from. Tear up the horoscope
that lied. Tell the online astrologers access
is denied, make them take you off the mailing list.

None of them predicted this.
The listening, listening to the restless house.
Unlock the door and there it is, the sound
you almost missed, the hiss
in and out, of breathing, the small sigh
the chair makes when you sit in it, the clock
that tells you every second of every hour.

Follow the steps of moonlight to the bed,
stand at the very edge, pull back
the covers for it, and it will offer you its light,
its lap. Feel the white-hot kiss.

The unwritten bed

Not cotton sheets, but paper.
Our bodies are falling through pages

and pages of unwritten words.
I am holding you, the warmth

and weight of you,
through layer after silent layer.

We are dropping past windows
and as we pass, look in at passing lives.

We are looking at you
coming in and going out, putting down a bag

of oranges and peeling them,
your life passing.

I am drifting down
with snow to the dazzling space where time

is nothing, and there is only paper,
paper enough to start a conversation.

Recording uninterrupted

Here you are on a small screen, unchanged
by the camera you know is always there,

always yourself. You never shift
or tilt your head that way

the camera expects you to.
This is how you are, unposed.

This is who you are,
seven years ago, or five, or three,

and you will always be
as young as this.

Here you speak to me,
reach across the camera,

your voice drowned out
by rustling sheets

and then the screen is bleached
white linen

and then the sound is an exclamation,
and then the sound is someone laughing

and then the sound is a kind of whirring.

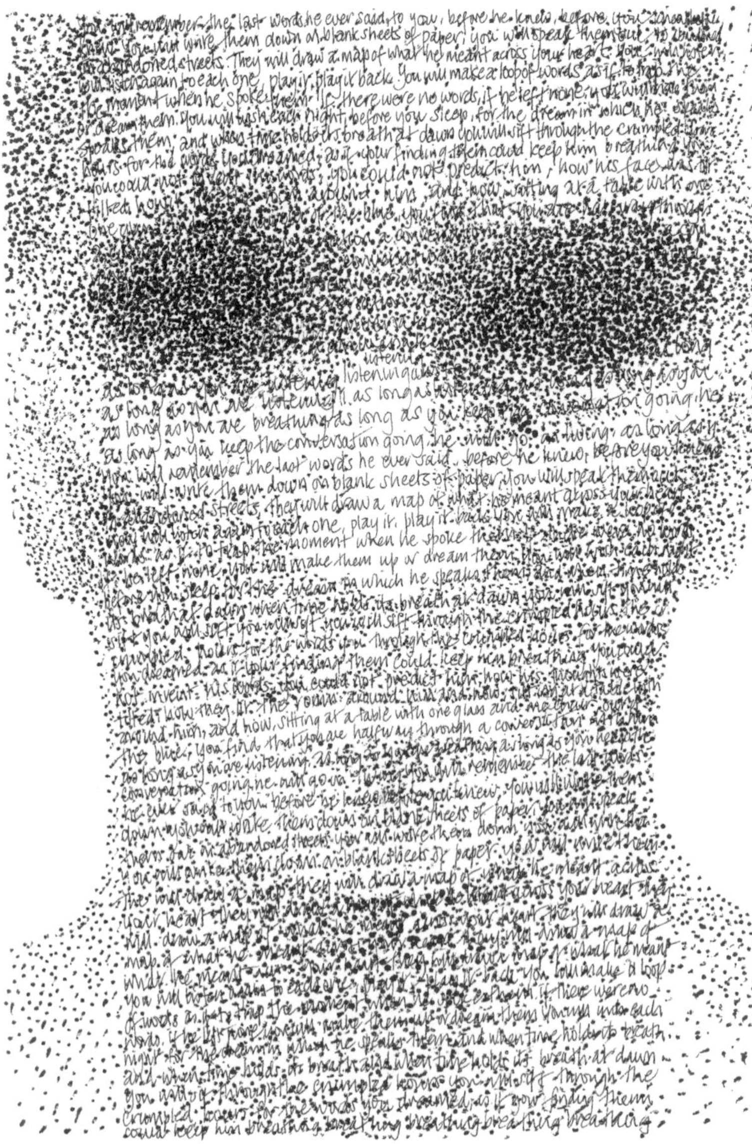

Murmuration

You are speaking in a flight of starlings,
in words that have the sheen of metal, a flash
of green or purple, an iridescence
on your tongue.

Starling words, once spoken, fly up
in swarms through a calm sky, through
the long light of evening,
and can never be unspoken or forgotten.

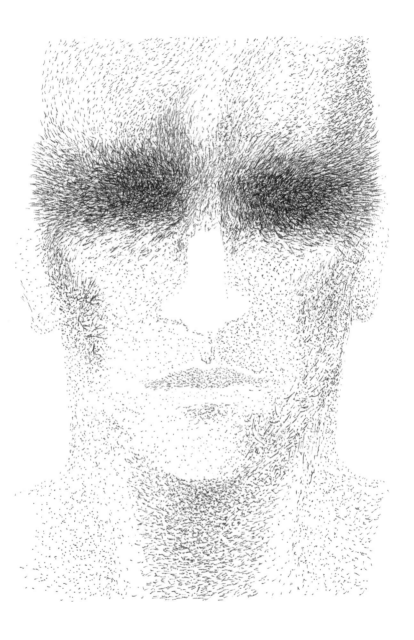

Passport photo

You come in to the photo booth, take off your smile,
untilt your head. As specified, the face

is straight, here is the signature and the date
that says you are forty, thirty, twenty-one.

A flare, a flash. With each one, the destination
changes. I watch you grow young.

The plastic walls remould themselves and melt
to snow, sunlight on a blinding shield of sea,

a sky burnt white beyond white
where anything is possible,

and you are standing on the edge
of the person you are about to be.

Out of this cramped space, this six-foot box,
when you are freed, where will you go,

over what seas, to what far islands?
After the siren songs and the lotus flesh,

the only kiss, the kiss of salt on your lips,
and the grain of your face thrown wide open,

how far will you go to look for home?

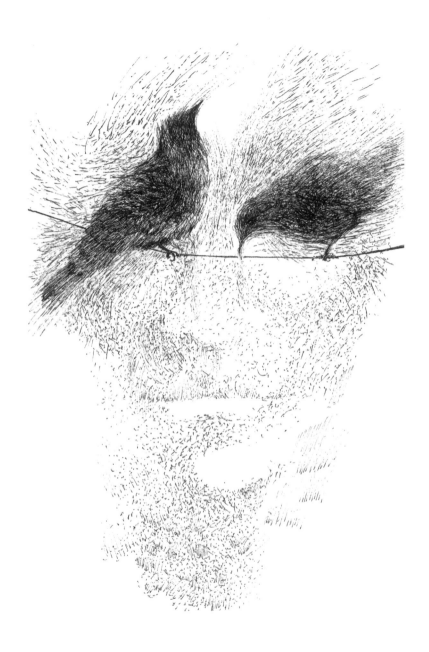

Disappeared

That look I recognise. The women's faces
have been cut away by scalpels of light,
pared so hard the person has disappeared.

White forehead, white cheekbones, black holes
where the eyes once were. They hold up the photographs
of husband, brother, son, the other disappeared.

They have turned the faces outward for everyone to see,
in case someone witnessed the nudge on the street
or saw them taken aside, or heard the knock on the door,

in case there is Information.
If they are speaking at all they are saying a name,
but all speech is lost in the wailing of sirens.

They hold up the faces of family men
who have been devoured on the usual road home
or swallowed whole by the exit door

and the photograph is a shield the women wear
over the heart, all the brightness turned outward
to where no one is looking, really, no one

is watching; towards a reason that may not be there,
really, a world that might as well have disappeared.

Threshold

There have been times
when you come in to a house
that sounds empty,

then suddenly come across him.
It is as if the sun and moon
come face to face

to clear the doubt
set up by silence, and devour
a desert's emptiness.

In the wilderness, Majnun
tears at his rags, lifts
his torn voice
against the booming
sky to shout,
I am here, I am waiting

and Laila, at the door
of a still house,
hesitates,

calls into the spidered gloom,
hoping he is there, asleep
in an inner room.

Late

The compartment is warm.
Outside is nothing but thin rain
and the moon, shivering.

I pick up my phone and put it down.

At the end of the line
is only a dark window, and in it
the face that does not wait
or speak.

It doesn't matter if the train is late.

Ephemeral

On the back window of the bus
a girl is writing on her breath

the disappearing message,
YES.

It takes no more than a breath
to blow the glass

out of a window-frame.
The sky screams in.

Birds like brooches on its chest,
it breaks

on the raised stick of the lunatic.
The desert turns

electric. Majnun, driven mad
with love, is blinded,

saying Laila's name.
The lightning offers advice.

Here, take this stick and write,
and he is writing, writing in the sand.

(Untitled)

The heart has become a fakir.
It has no pride, walks
naked, desires nothing,
is content to live on crumbs.

Spin

I meant to tell you about the silence
of birch trees, white against green,
not waiting for anything.

Instead we spoke about music,
the colour of it, and the unwritten
time between

where a hummingbird makes the world
stand still, and dancers spin
like mathematicians in love.

My steps are echoing through
empty rooms. This is not true.
The rooms are not empty

if I am walking through
them in search of you. The cycle begins
with one and ends with one,

dha dhin dhin dha, dha dhin dhin dha,
but the space between the beats is clean
and does not expect to be filled in.

Palimpsest

How to live again, when all the finished words
have been scraped off to leave the parchment clean.
How to come back willing for new events
to be scratched on old skin, to be reused
in unforeseen languages,

to be spread on a table under infrared
and inch by inch be studied, screened,
stripped down to the subtext. Ultraviolet
looks through the layers to the thing

they mean, the last flake of ink embedded
in a single thread, something holding on
to nothing, speech holding on to silence,
one mark holding on to the abyss

as if all life depended on it.

When the copperplate cracks

(Theatrum Orbis Terrarum)

So this is how it is done, one hand inching
round the coast to map its ins and outs,
to mark the point where ink may kiss
the river's mouth, or blade make up
a *terra incognita*, an imagined south.

This is where the needle turns to seek
a latitude, where acid bites the naked shore
and strips the sea till it is nothing
more than metallic light. The lived terrain
comes face to face with its mirror image

on the page, the world made up
and made again from sheets of ore, slept in,
loved in, tumbled, turned until the copper
buckles. You see it clearly in the print,
the place where metal

has been wounded, mended, where the hand
attempts to heal the breakline in the heart.

Kozo

If the intention is to raise the dead,
attention must be paid to every follicle,
every pore, every thread.

Examine the body, hidden for too long
in the secret, sacred room. It lies here,
scarred, perhaps beyond redemption,

scored by beetles, larvae, silverfish.
The proper spatula must be used to lift away
the grit and sand. Be aware the inks

are vulnerable and may not withstand
the treatment. You want these pages alive,
the crumpled skin smoothed flat, tears wiped

away with kozo tissue, beaten down
to be thin as a prayer, to repair the surface
layer by cobwebbed layer. This

is how resurrection looks. Not a sudden
blinding light and open arms and eyes cast up.
Here the eyes are concentrated

like a surgeon's, like a mother's, downward.

Digital

When you reach up and take them off the shelves,
the notebooks surrender, along with lists of specimens,
mineral, plant, animal, a treasury of smells.

This is quite distinct from the almond scent
of equations and astronomy,
or even the sage top note of calculus.

These letters on the other hand, unfolded,
let out a sigh of fading ink and smoke
from rooms where coal fires have been lit.

Sometimes you come across a trace
of the writer's or the reader's hand,
a smear of plum or pomegranate juice,

and from the deposit or the stain,
forensic science could probably isolate
the dna, and assign each one a name.

When you touch something you are changing it.

You touch me and I change.

But the manuscripts are rare and have to learn
self-preservation. They have to teach
themselves a way to live without the touch

and there it is, a sound more like a beak
on shell, a tap, a click. It hatches on a breath
and sends itself out to the world.

You touched me and I changed.

Gravitation may feel different in Kanpur,
the scribbled notes arrive more eucalyptus
to the scholar in Shanghai.

You touched me and I changed,
and when the touch is gone
am I diminished?

Or am I grown?

Nefertiti in the prison block

It could be polished ivory, minutely worked and delicate.
The head of an Egyptian queen, fit to be kept
under glass in a museum, an ancient work of art.

But look at it more closely. It turns out this is made
of matchsticks, packed tight and perfect, constructed
out of empty days and patience, stick by tiny stick,

made exquisite by this: that time is white
as bone when time is all you own and all
that can be done is to assemble it

unstruck, unburnt,
stick by stick
by stick

Trace

The woman with three plastic bags
gets off at King's Cross. I take her place
and sit uneasily in the heat she has left behind
The woman is a stranger and I mind
that she has been here in this seat
and that I have had to become aware
of her body, how recently she occupied
my space, how I took her place
too soon.

Thinking of moving, on the half-turn
between discomfort and irritation,
out of the tube-lit underground
I roll over into Sunday morning light
and the space you have left in the bed,
the scent of you coming off the sheets.
Like Majnun in the desert, thirsting,
I drink you in.

My body lets me sink
back into the warmth of her,
to feel a kind of gratitude for the remaining
trace, a message sent and just received.
I remember her face.

Screen-saver

I carry your face in a mobile shrine
and take it out on the Underground.

Your digital eyes look into mine.
I change at Farringdon and I have changed.

Touched by you, my skin is kozo tissue,
my hair rose-perfumed ink,

my eyelids are gold leaf.
The woman on my right,

reflected in the window opposite,
takes on the stillness of an icon,

the boy across the way
lifts his cheek to be pure marble

sculpted in living light. Together,
we travel on into the night,

all of us grown precious,
each one of us alive and rare.

The white room is white even in the dark and at its moonlit door someone is kn
that time of night when time stands still, when every sound is crystal, all the listeners
listening to the air that comes alive and crackles This is London calling, London calling, t
that cracks wide open, its winds rising, tides falling, and arrowed stars all pointing to th
to the face of a girl with a bullet in her head, her heart intent on learning, to the face of
a woman locked into a room half a world away, who has found this way, this way to look
face and say to me that she was listening when listening gave her hope that the knock on
there anybody there? need not mean fear and that a promise would be kept because somebod
listening in a throng of languages and rooms turned luminous. In spite of running feet and brea
someone was still praying, someone was saying
There were people laughing and air ris
our sweetheart was still singing
goodnight boys goodnight go
We'll meet again, don't know
know where, don't know wh
We'll meet again, don't kno
when we stop in the quiet
stop at the very start of
the heart meets its own g
and hears itself knocking
at the door of a whi

124

The Conversation

You will remember the last words he ever said
to you, before he knew, before you knew.
You will write them down on blank sheets
of paper, you will speak them out
to abandoned streets.

They will draw a map of what he meant
across your heart. You will listen again
to each one, play it, play it back. You will make
a loop of words as if to trap the moment
when he spoke them.

If there were no words, if he left none,
you will make them up or dream them.
You will wish each night, before you sleep,
for the dream in which
he speaks them,

and when time holds its breath at dawn,
you will sift through the crumpled hours
for the words you dreamed, as if
your finding them could keep him
breathing.

You could not invent his words,
you could not predict him,
how his smile was tilted, how
it lit the room
around him

and how, sitting at a table
with one glass and one chair,
out of nowhere you find that you
are halfway through a conversation
with him.

As long as you are listening,
as long as you are breathing,
as long as you keep the conversation going,
he will go on living.

I swear

Because I turned up from Bombay
too prissy to be rude
because you arrived via Leeds and Burnley
you thought it would do me good

to learn some Language. So

you never just fell, you went arse over tits,
and you were never not bothered
you just couldn't be arsed, and when
you laughed you laughed like an effing drain
and when there was pain it was a pain
in the arse.

That was just the start: you taught me
all the Language you knew
right through the alphabet from a to z,
from first to last, from bad to worse and worser
and the very worst you could muster.

I learned the curses. I learned the curser.
So proper you looked in your nice shoes and suit
until you produced Language like magic
out of your mouth and I was impressed

and oh I fell for you arse over tits
and when I said so you laughed like a drain
and we blinded and swore like the daft buggers
we were, all the way down Clerkenwell
and all the way up on the train
to the Horseshoe Pass.

And I tell you, since you went it's a pain
in the arse, and when some days I feel like shit
or when I say that I feel flat, I swear
I hear you laugh like a drain.
Not just flat, Mrs, Flat as a witch's tit,
that's what you say. Flat

as a witch's tit.

Swing

There is nothing
more than a swing-

door between living
and dying.

You have mastered
the art, half-

in, half-out,
time's magician,

of spinning something
out of nothing.

You conjure seven years
out of seven days, seven moons

out of half a song.
I've got the hang

of this, you say,
This dying

lark, and here
you are, living

as hard as you humanly
can, all the way to dying.

You set the door swinging
so fast I don't know

if I am coming
or going,

spun out to thin air
or reeled back

to your mouth
for the kiss

that denies we are dying,
dying on the way

to living
or living
on the way to dying,

and we are laughing
so hard we can't tell any more,

meri jaan, cariad,
we can't tell

if we are laughing
or crying.

Swan for Christmas

Most poets are swans
BUKOWSKI

It was you who told me about the starving
man and his two friends, shivering through winter
in a dingy room. He set out on Christmas Eve to find
a swan. Swan, goose, turkey, it was all the same
to him. Just imagine the man, his heart shaking,
climbing the park gate, lurking in the bushes
by the lake, lying in wait for its stately arrival.

How did he catch it? Easy, an unsuspecting swan,
expecting to be fed. It must have caught on at last,
fought back, bitten him black and blue. What a commotion
that must have been, the screaming bird and its furious mate,
a great clatter of wings. After he had wrung its beautiful neck,
how did he hide it, carry it back? In a shiny black
bin-bag, I expect.

One swan left behind in the icy Serpentine. One
would do fine, more than enough to feed the friends.
Carted home in a bus,

plucked, roasted, eaten. Afterwards,
the man sat back, a good host, his guests fed.
He wiped his mouths and told a few jokes.
That was where your story ended. But now I think
that after the hot dinner and the long evening,
just as he was about to turn in, the swan inside
began to sing. Inside all three, the sweetest voices,
in harmony, began to sing.

The song was not invisible.
The song was white feathers
floating from their mouths
into the frozen air.
Across the city at the lake,
the lover stopped his furious searching,
hushed his great wings and listened
to the sky crying
white tears.

The three
lifted their faces to feathers,
a benediction of snow
or feathers, it didn't matter which,
snow or feathers, feathers or snow,
swans or poets, poets or swans,
it came to the same thing.

Invisible

My beak is a knife in the heart of the moon,
my wings attack the stricken lake. The sky
a war-zone of feathers, I stake out what was
our territory, hiss at unwary passers-by.

This world has gone wrong. One reflection
where there must be two, the skin of the water torn
when I stab and stab again to look for you, forgetting
for an instant, knowing, wishing not to know

my own image in the grieving water. You
show me this. Look at us, you say, look at me in you.
This is who we are. This is how we live,
coming and going through each other.

My eyes turn silver,
our reflection in the sparkled water
and the moon, thrilled.

Passing

There is a kind of splendour in these northbound trains
when the evening fades along the tracks, and stations
grow elegant under the veil of rain.

Concourses and overbridges find their glamour
as daylight fades and lights spark on. At Crewe,
I turn away from the platform's glitter

to the window opposite, past my ghost reflection
in the spangled glass, and see you
in another train, arriving at the junction

as if you were expected. No surprise
to find you there, the wing of hair,
the tilted head. Your eyes

torch into me as if I were a well
or tunnel that needed you to light me up
and make me visible again. All

the stations throw away their names,
the gods of trains give up their destinations,
our timetables spin and overlap. Frame

locks on frame, a double exposure,
the interior of my carriage cast over yours
in an algebra of darkness and disclosure,

as though some architect has plotted this,
the intricacy of jali on an ancient tomb,
the pattern of your birthmark on my wrist.

Our images lie over each other,
like two people who have been granted
another lifetime to be lovers.

No need to press my face against the pane
or lift a hand as my train leaves, as yours
sets off. Reflections clasp and part and dazzle

and we are windows passing windows passing
passing windows passing passing windows
passing windows in the rain.

1977

(I am quite sure of this)

Some Glaswegians still speak of the Silver Jubilee
and the Queen's cavalcade sailing off
from George Square on a sea of Union Jacks.
Others recall that around the same time
the Sex Pistols' *God Save the Queen*
was black-listed by the BBC

      but what I remember is
      that one night I danced in sequined
      hotpants, with a boy in polyester
      flares (I am quite sure of this),
      in time, on track, one hand in the air,
      one step forward, one step back.

Time is easily tangled. It falls over its own feet.
That year peeled itself away perfectly
and they say smallpox was eradicated,
miles of fibre optics laid, personal computers
offered to the masses.
People said it had never been so good

      but what I remember is
      the popcorn mix at Regal Cinema,
      salt over sweet, the triumph of good
      over evil, light-sabres slashing the air
      in synchronised time. In time, on track,
      one step forward, one step back.

People said it had never been so bad,
Bengal hit by a cyclone, snow in Miami,

New York plunged into darkness
and out of the sky a fireball fell on Innisfree.
People said it was a sign. And that was the year
Steve Biko died.

Other people died in other years, but that year
Groucho Marx and Charlie Chaplin died.
Jacques Prévert and Robert Lowell died.
In Memphis, Elvis died. Still,
someone called Roy Sullivan was struck
by lightning for the seventh time
and survived

> but because of the odd way time unfolds,
> what I remember is the last few seconds,
> the countdown under a glitterball
> (I am quite sure of this),
> light flashing in your eyes
> and your hair as you moved
> in time, on track, one hand in the air,
> one step forward, one step back,

and *ah ah ah ah*
staying alive, staying alive.

Ah ah ah ah
staying alive.

Litter

At Derby station
on the pavement where you stood
I leave your shoes.

At Sheffield
in the café where you sat
I leave the orange scarf.

On the Liverpool ferry
I leave your overcoat
by the freezing rail

where you pointed out
Hope Street.
On Hope Street

at the traffic lights
between the two cathedrals,
I leave your photograph.

On the platform
at Euston, your suitcase
with green tags.

At the front door
I leave grieving.
Coming in, I say your name.

Saying your name, I bring you home.

Say his name

Not standing by graves.

Say his name in conversation,
at tables where glasses are raised.

Say his name where you live,
in the company of friends.

Listening

The white room is white even in the dark
and at its moonlit door someone is knocking

at that time of night when time is crystal,
all the listeners
listening

listening
to the air that comes alive and crackles
This is London calling

to a space that cracks wide open,
its winds rising, its tides falling

and arrowed stars all pointing
to the face of the traveller huddled at the door,

to the face of a girl with a bullet in her head,
her heart set on learning,

to the face of a woman locked into a room
half a world away, who has found this way
to look into my face and say to me that she was
listening

when listening
gave her hope that the knock on the door
Is there anybody there? need not mean fear

and that a promise would be kept
because somebody was
listening

the white room is white even in the dark and at its moonlit door someone is kn
that time of night when time stands still, when every sound is crystal, all the listeners
listening to the air that comes alive and crackles this is London calling, London calling,
that cracks wide open, its winds rising, tides falling, and arrowed stars all pointing to th
to the face of a girl with a bullet in her head, her heart intent on learning, to the face of
a woman locked into a room half a world away, who has found this way, this way to boo
face and say to me that she was listening when listening gave her hope that the knock on
there anybody there? Need not mean fear and that a promise would be kept because somebod
listening in a throng of languages and rooms turned luminous. In spite of running feet and brea
someone was still praying, someone was sayin   someone was saying don't panic do
There were people laughing and ar   at our door our sweetheart was s
our sweetheart was still singing   singing singing singing sing
goodnight boys goodnight   don't know whe
we'll meet again, don't kno   don't know w
know where, don't know   where, don
We'll meet again, don't k   stop at the
When we stop in the quiet   at the
stop at the very start of   the heart
the heart meets its own   heart meet
and hears itself knockin   heart well
at the door of a white

142

listening
in a throng of languages and rooms turned luminous.

In spite of running feet and breaking glass,
someone was still praying. Someone was saying
Don't panic. Don't panic.

There were people laughing
and at our door, our sweetheart was still singing,
*Goodnight boys, goodnight. We'll meet again,
don't know where, don't know when.*

When we stop in the quiet moonlight, stop

at the very start of silence,
the heart meets its own language
and hears itself
knocking

knocking
at the door of a white room
that is white even in the dark, and even the dark
is listening.

Fair copy

(on reading the notebooks of Siegfried Sassoon)

Ten years old. Your gift to Mamsy is
the book of poems you have laboured over,
illustrated, written out fair with a frontispiece,
a contents page and then the wise old lines,
much older than you are. You have hardly lived,
but the loss you write is real as a person.
Long before he is due, the Reaper appears.

What did you know about being disconsolate?
At ten, you planned your book, took pleasure
in being in command. Here at the end
of the page you instruct your only intended reader
as if it would never occur to her, *Turn over.*
She must have smiled and turned and admired
your skill, pretending not to notice

when you lifted a line from an older, wearier poet.
It was much later that the desolation
became your own, not borrowed. Your boys,
your brother, your friends the poets gone.
It was later that you bled. In the hospital
they worked over you, wrote you out fair
and sent you home, whole. Here's the tag to prove it,

and you are writing over and over a trench
in pencil until the lines seem worth saving,
and then you write over the pencil in ink to say
they are worth saying. You weigh a word, cut
a phrase, erase a verse. When you think
you have quite healed them, you give them a tag
and send them away

but at the end of a corrected page,
there is a hesitation as if you are waiting
for the instruction, *Turn over*,
as if you are on the verge of writing
the words that refuse to be written.

A century later

The school-bell is a call to battle,
every step to class, a step into the firing-line.
Here is the target, fine skin at the temple,
cheek still rounded from being fifteen.

Surrendered, surrounded, she
takes the bullet in the head

and walks on. The missile cuts
a pathway in her mind, to an orchard
in full bloom, a field humming under the sun,
its lap open and full of poppies.

This girl has won
the right to be ordinary,

wear bangles to a wedding, paint her fingernails,
go to school. *Bullet*, she says, *you are stupid.*
You have failed. You cannot kill a book
or the buzzing in it.

A murmur, a swarm. Behind her, one by one,
the schoolgirls are standing up
to take their places on the front line.

Drummer

The pavement is a drum beneath your feet.

When you return as usual, crossing the square,
walking down the familiar street,
you need no signposts to take you home.
You feel the hum of buses, trains booming
underground, strong and close as your own
heartbeat.

Drummer, you know these thoroughfares,
you have played them. These roads
lay claim to you.

So when the blade meets skin,
the whole street stops, feels the sting.
Hack at you, and the city bleeds.

Even in broad daylight, the alleys
turn dark and glitter with long knives,
but the nightmare cannot hold you in.
You fall out of it. You fall back
into the city's sickened heart,
and it beats harder, begins to speak
in every language, deep down
where the blood thunders

Not in my name. Not in my name.
the city's heart becomes a drum,
dhak dhak, dhak dhak, dhak dhak.
It speaks the name you understand,
the difficult name, the name of peace.

Midnight, Christmas Eve

So simple, on a night like this, to lose
all fear and lean too far out on the bridge
in admiration of the stars that throw
themselves into black water

and disappear. From the river's edge
a song begins, flung up from the cathedral,
lifted through its ribs of stone
past its candled arches and its domes

to icy sky, a sound that feels
as pure, unreal as snow falling upward.
The portal is thrown open with the force
of something that wants to be alive.

Song like this could spark a fire
from hopeless wood, or give birth
out of stricken earth to forests
of branch and leaf and bud.

Across the city, a girl's hair swings
against her cheek, her hands feel
kicking feet, a heartbeat.
The great vault with all its singing

swoops down to look, to where she looks,
a cathedral turned to cradle, the cradle
a gently ribbed cathedral, deep as the sky,
starlit, ready to be filled.

London Bells

A morning full of bells,
Mary-le-Bow, St Bartholomew-the-Great,

St Paul's, St Giles Cripplegate,
enough bells to make you believe

in Christmas. You want to tell
this sound in ink, witness it on paper,

stand on the brink of belief
and look in.

When the bells fall silent,
the silence is well-deep, well dropped

into the rubbled heart. You could start
to believe there is a day

when screens go to their saver
and over the Millennium Bridge,

sheep come in to be a flock
and keep the faith.

A sacred day. Trucks
leave the roads clear for the magi.

A child is born and a mother counts
its fingers, thinking
This is miracle enough for me.

First words

(for Ava)

Her fingers scrabble at glass,
over floorboards, table legs and chairs
to catch the word that runs away from her,
sifted through leaves, snatched up on a breeze,
stolen by clouds, returned.

Propelled on bottom, elbows, knees,
with silent determination, she follows it
and only when it spills out of her hand,
whispers, like someone in a church
or library, *sunshine.*

She knows the moon even when
it is nothing more than a curl on blue,
or half an ear listening for the next star.
Even the disc of milk in a bowl is *moon.*
She says the word and drinks it in.

One foot

(for Luca Simon Powell)

Out of the Moses basket where it rocks,
your foot appears, resolute, as if
you are stepping into air,
treading it like water.

This foot is so unused, so new the light
shines through. It does not know
what ground is, the dangerous play
as earth turns round and falls

away, the hurt of tumbling down.
It walks, unafraid, into the time
between my heartbeats. The man
whose name you wear

made room for you. He was there,
measuring the length and width of things,
one shoe in front of the other,
heel to toe, heel to toe,

foot by foot by foot. Space enough
for hills and circling arms, and for you
to map the distance of your name.
Then he left the floor to you,

to measure in your own good time,
a floor that looks like love, like air,

and you are stepping on to it.

ACKNOWLEDGEMENTS:

Some of these poems first appeared in *To the Moon*, ed. Carol Ann Duffy (Picador, 2009); *Jubilee Lines*, ed. Carol Ann Duffy (Faber, 2012); *The Yellow Nib Modern English Poetry by Indians*, ed. Sudeep Sen (The Seamus Heaney Centre for Poetry, Queen's University Belfast, 2012); *1914: Poetry Remembers*, ed. Carol Ann Duffy (Faber, 2013); *The Twelve Poems of Christmas*, ed. Carol Ann Duffy (Candlestick Press, 2013); *Moving Worlds: A Journal of Transcultural Writings*, 'Postcolonial Cities: South Asia' special issue, ed. Dr Caroline Herbert (2013); *The Hundred Years' War: modern war poems*, ed. Neil Astley (Bloodaxe Books, 2014).

Acknowledgements are also due to Thresholds Poets in Residence 2013 Cambridge; *The Guardian*; BBC World Service (The Forum); The National Gallery; London Lines, the Southbank Centre; The Healing Swaying compiled for performance by Piers Plowright and Stephen Tucker.

I would like to thank Carol Ann Duffy and Gillian Clarke, who caused many of these poems to be written; Simon Armitage, John Agard, Grace Nichols, Jackie Kay, Glyn Maxwell, Peter Buckroyd and Tony Childs, who knew Simon Powell longer than I did, for all the conversations, ideas shared over bread and wine, and strange meetings at railway stations; Daljit Nagra, Caroline Bird, Joe Dunthorne, Lemn Sissay, Moniza Alvi, Arundhathi Subramaniam, Choman Hardi for enlightenment in unlikely places, from Tungha in Colombia to the Animal Garden in Nairobi to Hull Station; Helen Taylor of Thresholds, who gave me precious time as Poet in Residence at the Cambridge University Library with Anne Jarvis, John Wells, Marjolein Allen, Jim Bloxam, Emma Saunders, Stuart Stone, Adam Perkins, Anne Taylor, Ed Potten and Yasmin Faghihi; the students and staff of the Thomas Deacon Academy, Peterborough, and the Linton

Village School for teaching me things I didn't know; Gertraud Ekama, for correcting my imaginary German; Judith Chernaik, Cicely Herbert, Gerard Benson, Emily Kasriel, Radek Boschetty, Emma Harding, Kate Howells, Maggie Fergusson, Isobel Abulhoul, Gabriel Griffin, Anna Dreda, Naomi Jaffa, Maggie Robertson, William Ayot, Juliet Grayson, Mark Hewitt, Graham Henderson, Sophie Wardell, Jude Kelly, Bea Colley, Anna Selby, Julia Bird, for growing the spaces for poetry; Sonia and John Broadbent, for taking me back to the blackberries; Hannah Andrassey and her family Steve Escritt, Polly and Lexie; Rita McGrath, Sean McGrath, Rachel and Michael Dwyer; In India, Monika and Charles Correa, Uma and Gerson da Cunha, Bakul Patel, Beena Chadda; Vicky Edwards and Stella Fearnley of Poetry Live; everyone at Bloodaxe, Neil Astley, Simon Thirsk, Christine Macgregor, Suzanne Fairless-Aitken, Rebecca Hodkinson, Bethan Jones, Jean Smith, Alison Davis, as well as Pamela Robertson-Pearce. Special thanks to Iwan, Gareth and Daniel Powell, Lucia Yandoli, Becky Gilbey; my family in Glasgow, Iqbal and Nosheena Mobarik; Shahnaz and Jim Lambert; my family in Wales, Jean Powell, Nick and Carys Powell, Shon and Lesley Powell, Ianto and Sarah Carvell-Powell; Robert Taylor, Ayesha Dharker Taylor for being the most patient of listeners; Ava Taylor and Luca Simon Powell for the continuation.

Imtiaz Dharker was born in Lahore, Pakistan, grew up a Muslim Calvinist in a Lahori household in Glasgow and was adopted by India and married into Wales. She is an accomplished artist and documentary film-maker, and has published five collections with Bloodaxe in Britain, all including her own drawings: *Postcards from god* [including *Purdah*] (1997), *I speak for the devil* (2001), *The terrorist at my table* (2006) *Leaving Fingerprints* (2009) and *Over the Moon* (2014). She was awarded the Queen's Gold Medal for Poetry 2014 for *Over the Moon* and in recognition of a lifetime's commitment to poetry.